LUNAR NEW YEAR

DiscoverRoo
An Imprint of Pop!
popbooksonline.com

Susan E. Hamen

abdobooks.com

Published by Pop!, a division of ABDO, PO Box 398166, Minneapolis, Minnesota 55439. Copyright © 2021 by POP, LLC. International copyrights reserved in all countries. No part of this book may be reproduced in any form without written permission from the publisher. Pop!™ is a trademark and logo of POP, LLC.

Printed in the United States of America, North Mankato, Minnesota.

052020
092020

THIS BOOK CONTAINS
RECYCLED MATERIALS

Cover Photo: Shutterstock Images
Interior Photos: Shutterstock Images, 1, 6, 8–9, 11, 14, 15, 23, 24, 25, 27, 28, 29, 31; Visual China Group/Getty Images, 5, 30; Mark Schiefelbein/AP Images, 7; iStockphoto, 12, 18 (top), 18 (bottom), 21; Gary Chuah/AP Images, 13; Vichan Poti/Pacific Press/Sipa USA/AP Images, 16; Yichuan Cao/Sipa USA/AP Images, 17; Rio V. De Sieux, 19 (top); Imagine China/Newscom, 19 (bottom); Chinatopix/AP Images, 22

Editor: Connor Stratton
Series Designer: Jake Slavik

Content Consultant: Zhao Ma, PhD, Associate Professor of Modern Chinese History and Culture, Washington University in St. Louis

Library of Congress Control Number: 2019955009
Publisher's Cataloging-in-Publication Data
Names: Hamen, Susan E., author.
Title: Lunar New Year / by Susan E. Hamen
Description: Minneapolis, Minnesota : POP!, 2021 | Series: Cultural celebrations | Includes online resources and index.
Identifiers: ISBN 9781532167706 (lib. bdg.) | ISBN 9781532168802 (ebook)
Subjects: LCSH: New Year--Juvenile literature. | Lunar calendars--Juvenile literature. | Holidays--Juvenile literature. | Social customs--Juvenile literature.
Classification: DDC 394.261--dc23

WELCOME TO DiscoverRoo!

Pop open this book and you'll find QR codes loaded with information, so you can learn even more!

Scan this code* and others like it while you read, or visit the website below to make this book pop!

popbooksonline.com/lunar-new-year

*Scanning QR codes requires a web-enabled smart device with a QR code reader app and a camera.

TABLE OF CONTENTS

CHAPTER 1
AT THE PARADE

A huge crowd lines a street. Floats pass by as music plays. The floats are decorated with flowers and paper lanterns. People with poles carry a

WATCH A VIDEO HERE!

Several people hold up each dragon costume. They work together to make the dragon dance.

dragon costume. The dragon swoops

and turns. People are celebrating the

Lunar New Year.

Fireworks are a common part of Lunar New Year celebrations.

People celebrate Lunar New Year

around the world. It is most popular in

Asia, especially in China. The holiday

marks the beginning of spring. People prepare for luck and happiness in the new year.

DID YOU KNOW?

More than one billion people around the world celebrate Lunar New Year.

Performers often drum during Lunar New Year.

Lunar New Year takes place at the

beginning of the **lunar calendar**. The

lunar calendar is based on the phases of

Lunar New Year begins on a new moon. A new moon is when the moon appears to be dark.

the moon. It is different from a standard

calendar. Standard calendars are based

on the position of the sun.

CHAPTER 2
HISTORY OF LUNAR NEW YEAR

Thousands of years ago, many people in China farmed. To tell time, farmers studied the moon. When spring was coming, people celebrated Lunar New Year. They offered **sacrifices** to gods and

LEARN MORE HERE!

People in ancient China wrote down events and created early calendars on tortoise shells and oracle bones.

ancestors. Farmers hoped they would

bring good fortune and health.

Followers of **Buddhism** began

lighting lanterns at least 2,000 years ago.

The lanterns honored the religion's main

teacher, Buddha. Between 206 BCE and

220 CE, the practice started spreading.

It became known as the Lantern Festival.

This festival marked

the end of Lunar

New Year.

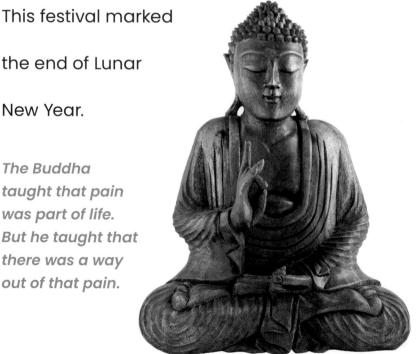

The Buddha taught that pain was part of life. But he taught that there was a way out of that pain.

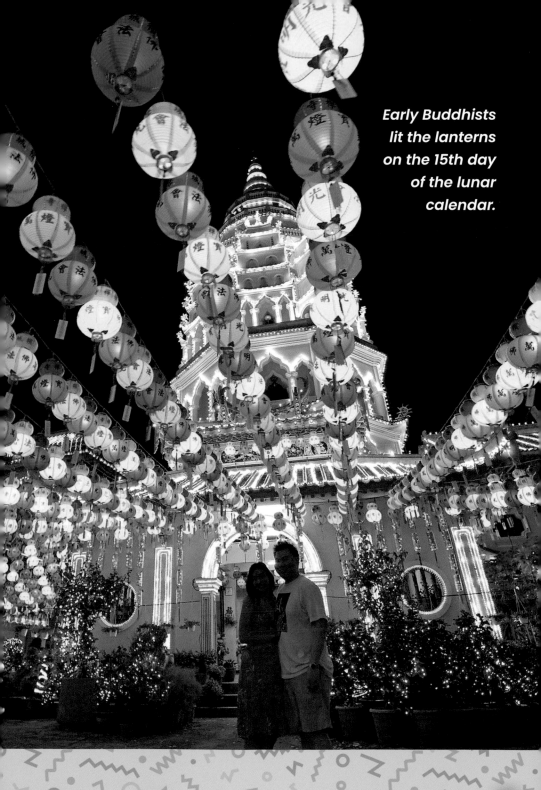

Early Buddhists lit the lanterns on the 15th day of the lunar calendar.

Dragons are important to many central stories of Chinese culture. Dragons are thought to be kind protectors.

By the 200s CE, people had also begun performing dragon dances and lion dances. Dragon dances honored people's ancestors. They tried to bring rain for the harvest too. Lion dances represented a beast known as Nian. Over time, these dances became part of Lunar New Year.

Today, Lunar New Year is popular in South Korea, Vietnam, Thailand, Cambodia, and Malaysia.

After 220 CE, the holiday became more social. Families had feasts. They lit firecrackers. They gave gifts of money in red envelopes. Lunar New Year spread across Asia. Chinese people also moved around the world. They brought the holiday with them.

The United States is home to some of the largest Lunar New Year celebrations outside of Asia.

DID YOU KNOW?

In China, Lunar New Year is also called the Spring Festival.

LUNAR NEW YEAR TIMELINE

1600s BCE
Lunar New Year begins among farmers in China. Farmers make sacrifices to ancestors and gods.

800s CE
People in China invent gunpowder and fireworks.

206 BCE-220 CE
The Lantern Festival and dragon dance become popular in China.

1910s

Lunar New Year begins to be called the Spring Festival in China. The country's new government makes it a national holiday. This government was led by Yuan Shikai.

2010s

People start sending digital red envelopes for Lunar New Year. Apps such as WeChat become popular during the celebration.

给你发了一个红包

恭喜发财，大吉大利

開

CHAPTER 3
TRADITIONS

Lunar New Year has many **traditions**.
Before the holiday, people often clean
their homes. Cleaning helps sweep bad
luck out. People also decorate homes,

LEARN MORE HERE!

People often hang red lanterns during Lunar New Year.

shops, and streets with red. This color

stands for luck and joy.

Every year, hundreds of millions of people travel to be with their families for Lunar New Year.

In China, people get time off for the holiday. So, many people return to their hometowns. Families have dinner on the night before Lunar New Year begins. People eat foods such as fish, dumplings,

spring rolls, and noodles. But the meal

changes from place to place. In South

Korea, people often eat rice cake soup.

Families often eat lucky foods during Lunar New Year.

The **Chinese Zodiac** is another part of Lunar New Year. Each Lunar New Year celebrates the animal sign of that year. People often buy decorations with the new year's zodiac animal.

In the Chinese Zodiac, 2020 was the Year of the Rat.

THE CHINESE ZODIAC

The Chinese Zodiac has 12 animals. An animal stands for each year. After 12 years, the animals repeat.

CHAPTER 4
THE LANTERN FESTIVAL

Lunar New Year lasts for 16 days. The final

night of holiday is the Lantern Festival.

The festival happens on the first full moon

night in the **lunar calendar**. It marks the

COMPLETE AN ACTIVITY HERE!

return of spring. The Lantern Festival also

represents families coming together.

Lunar New Year lanterns are often made
with paper.

In Vietnam, people float flower-shaped lanterns on water.

People light lanterns for many

reasons, such as honoring **ancestors**.

Most places set off fireworks too.

People often eat sweet rice dumplings.

Performers do dragon and lion dances as well. The festival ends Lunar New Year by looking toward the future with hope.

Lanterns often have traditional Chinese images such as fruits, flowers, and birds.

MAKING CONNECTIONS

TEXT-TO-SELF

Families light lanterns during Lunar New Year. What is something your family does every year?

TEXT-TO-TEXT

Have you read books about other holidays? What do they have in common with Lunar New Year? How are they different?

TEXT-TO-WORLD

Lunar New Year started in China, but it spread around the world. Can you think of other holidays or practices that have spread from where they began?

GLOSSARY

ancestor – a family member who lived long ago.

Buddhism – a religion that began in India and spread across Asia, based on teachings that help people escape pain and desire.

Chinese Zodiac – a cycle of 12 years with an animal representing each one of those years.

lunar calendar – a system of organizing the year based on the phases of the moon.

sacrifice – an offering to a god or ancestor in order to receive protection or power.

tradition – a belief or way of doing things that is passed down from person to person over time.

INDEX

ONLINE RESOURCES
popbooksonline.com

Scan this code* and others like it while you read, or visit the website below to make this book pop!

popbooksonline.com/lunar-new-year

*Scanning QR codes requires a web-enabled smart device with a QR code reader app and a camera.